Jenny Drape
73 Christine
N. Ton, N.Y.

HORSES

BY PETER CHURCHILL

Cathay Books

CONTENTS

Spring comes to the country, and a solitary grey horse enjoys the sun as it waits for its human companions.

INTRODUCTION

Between 40 and 60 million years ago, a small, four-legged, pad-footed creature roamed in small herds over what is now the continent of North America. As the earth developed through the Oligocene and Miocene phases of its existence, so too did the early *Equus* family develop. Then in the Pliocene period, between ten and one million years ago, herds of primitive ponies started out on a long journey across now-extinct land bridges into Eurasia. These herds formed two important branches of the *Equus* family, the Hipparion and the Pliohippus. The Hipparion travelled on to the Far East and North Africa, while the Pliohippus became the first true soliped, an equus with solid hooves.

The world formed into continental land-masses that were divided from each other by natural barriers – oceans, mountains and deserts – thus concentrating many different types of animal life into six major zones. In one of them – the Ethiopian zone – there evolved the zebra of Africa, the wild ass and the onager (a half-ass, half-pony creature), all close cousins of the horse, while in the Palaearctic and Oriental zones varying types of wild pony developed.

We can get some idea of how those wild ponies may have looked from the Mongolian pony which still lives in both a feral and a domesticated state in Mongolia (see page 25).

Over the centuries, herds of horses and ponies established themselves in the Far East, India, the Asiatic steppes, the Middle East, North Africa, Spain, Northern and Southern Europe, and Great Britain. But the developing types could be divided into two basic ones: the Northern and Southern Horse. While there is no difference in the normal body temperature of both types, the Northern Horse, usually heavier and thicker skinned, was defined as cold-blooded, and the Southern Horse, being more agile and thinner-skinned, was defined as warm-blooded. From the Northern Horse have developed the heavy, draught-horse breeds

and the native pony breeds found in most countries of the world today, and from the Southern Horse have come the finer Arab, Barb, Standardbred, Saddlebred and Thoroughbred strains.

Where or when man first domesticated the horse is not really known, but it is fairly certain that the nomadic tribes that wandered over the Asiatic steppes about 2000 years ago were the first true horsemen and horsemasters of the world. While settled man was perfecting the complicated arts of building and agriculture, nomadic man was driving his herds of horses from one corner of Eurasia to another. Tribes of horse-trading Celts travelled all over the Old World, some as far afield as India and China, many of them settling in the various states to work as mercenaries and horse-trainers.

Among the earliest known pieces of evidence of horses being ridden are the impressions left by Assyrian artists. The Hittites and the Assyrians were the first organized cavalrymen, with thousands of well-disciplined charioteers and mounted men, and in the years around 1500 B.C., Kikkulis, a horse-master to the kings of the Hittites, recorded the first written laws governing horsemanship and stable management.

For the ancient Greeks, the horse was a rare, expensive and exotic animal. Most of Greece was rocky, mountainous and poor in pasture, but

---

Lipizzaners at their summer grazing quarters in the Austrian Alps. Although best known for their connections with the Spanish Riding School of Vienna, Lipizzaners are also used in agriculture in Yugoslavia and Bulgaria. These horses are of amiable character with strong, well-developed bodies and the traditional convex face. They can be of any colour but only the grey stallions are used by the highly trained riders of the Spanish Riding School.

horse-breeding thrived on the fertile plains of Thessaly, now modern Bulgaria. Alexander the Great's favourite horse, Bucephalus, was Thessalian-bred.

So far, the horse had been used mainly in warfare, although the ancient Persians enjoyed polo and horse-racing, and the Greeks introduced horse-racing and chariot racing into the original Olympic Games. The Romans, too, enjoyed chariot-racing, and with their superb roads, the horse began to play an ever-increasing role in transport and communications.

Up to this point in time, the ox and the ass were the principal beasts of burden. Oxen were harnessed to the earliest ploughs, for it was not until the invention of the horse-collar in the Middle Ages that the horse came into general use in agriculture.

The principle of the use of cavalry as the most effective means of waging war remained invincible for generations, through the Moors, the Mongols, the Normans and, with the development of heavy armour and longer weapons, the chivalrous medieval knights and their heavy horses.

Then, with the Renaissance, riding became an art, and *haute école* (high school) riding became one of the most popular forms of court entertainment in the countries of Europe throughout the 16th, 17th and 18th centuries. Living examples of these classical techniques of equitation can be seen today in the performances of the Spanish Riding School in Vienna, Austria, and the Cadre Noir at Saumur, in France.

During the great period of exploration of the sixteenth century, the horse was taken by man back to its original homeland, the Americas. Native Indian tribesmen of the plains had never seen horses, but they soon mastered the techniques of riding, and the Commanche in particular became some of the finest mounted warriors ever seen.

As techniques of warfare changed, so too did the various forms of equestrian sport. In the Middle Ages, jousting, hunting and hawking were the favourite pastimes of men of rank and opulence. But the first real sporting horse was to come in the shape of the sleek and highly sensitive Thoroughbred, a pure strain of horse developed in England for the sport of racing. Organized horse-racing first began in England in the reign of James I. Later, Charles II encouraged the importation of Eastern stallions to form the basis for the breeding of a racehorse.

Three stallions in particular entered the record books as the founding fathers of the Thoroughbred. These were the Byerley Turk, the Darley Arabian and the Godolphin Arabian. Their blood can be found in the male line of all Thoroughbreds, but to say that they created the Thoroughbred is to over-simplify a very complicated process. For in the breeding of racehorses, the various in-crosses and out-crosses are just as important as the more apparent sire and dam. Nevertheless, the blood of these Eastern stallions and their descendants, the great racehorses of the pre-twentieth century, still flows through the veins of the million-dollar 'racing machines' which draw vast crowds to the race-tracks today.

With the coming of mechanization and the industrial revolution, the horse retired from many of its traditional roles. But still today in the rugged countries of Central Europe, from the Balkans to the Black Sea, strong ponies, descended from the ancient steppe ponies and native strains of heavy draught horse, continue to work as pack-horses or as the most practical and economical source of motive power in agriculture. This is also the case in many other less developed regions of the world, Meanwhile, in the industrialized countries of the world, the stockmen, cowboys and soldiers directed their skills in the saddle to competition events. The Rodeo, with competitive events such as cutting-out and roping of steers, and bronco-riding, all based on the daily working life of the mounted cowboy, is now North America's second largest equestrian spectator sport and in Australia, barrel-racing and camp-drafting attract huge crowds at the state horse and agricultural shows.

The great era of the military riding academies like Saumur, Pinerole, Madrid, Weedon and West Point which reigned supreme in sporting equitation for the first half of this century contributed to the creation of the modern sports of three-day eventing and show jumping. ·

Since World War II, show jumping has grown into a major international sport with its own superstars and national teams from many countries now travel the international circuit to great shows. Great horses, too, have become superstars, like Britain's immortal Foxhunter and Pennwood Forge Mill, America's Idle Dice and the fabulous Jet Run.

Three-day eventing has been popular in continental Europe for many years, but now British and American riders have come right to the top of this demanding sport. Competition dressage, too, is more of a European sport, but its following in America, Britain and Australia is growing fast.

A superb American Anglo-Arab on a breeding station in Phoenix, Arizona. The Anglo-Arab is one of the finest riding horses in the world and is defined as a cross between a Thoroughbred stallion and an Arab mare or vice versa. There should be no other blood in the strain but Arab and Thoroughbred. Most countries of the world follow these rules but in the USA the breed must contain not less than 25% of Arab blood nor more than 75% Thoroughbred blood. The Anglo-Arab is very successful in combined training and showjumping.

HORSE LIFE

Horses lead two sorts of lives: the ones we organize for them, and the ones they organize for themselves. The inquisitive grey in its stable has all the details of its daily routine managed for it by its owner. In contrast, the mares and foal (*below*) on their stud-farm have much more day-to-day freedom. But they are still a very long way from living like horses in the wild. This does not mean, however, that they and all the other domestic horses of today do not live their lives to the full. They do – as long as they get all the care, affection and security that their human partners can give them.

Horseplay

Horses, when turned out in the paddock or living out on grass, will often roll (*below*). It is part of their natural instincts to keep their coats and skins healthy. Young horses will often roll just for the sheer fun of it. A young foal plays with its mother (*right*) although the mare seems to be ignoring it. In its wild state the horse was a hunted creature and its basic nature is that of a pacifist although stallions will occasionally fight over a mare. The well-grown foal on the left is nearly ready to take its place in the adult world of horses. Here the foal joins one of its seniors in a preening session. When living out on grass most horses need careful grooming, not just by their stable-mates but by their owners.

The horse is not by nature a fighter; it has no natural weapons like sharp teeth, horns, claws or even a threatening roar. But because of its timid and alert character it is by nature a very insecure creature. It is, as well, highly charged with jealousy, such as that between the two young colts (*far left*) as they begin to mature. Similar scenes are shown on a stud farm (*below*) and (*near left*) in the wild. It is very rare for horses to injure each other in these power struggles but with domesticated horses and ponies that are shod, leg injuries from kicking often result. In the wild, spirited young colts sometimes attempt to take the mares of the herds' stallion leader, thus provoking him.

Horse talk

Horses communicate with each other basically through smell and threatening postures. The neigh or whinny made through nostrils and mouth is primarily a call sign. A mare will call to her youngster should it stray too far away from her and a stallion will softly neigh through his nostrils as a form of recognition to his mares. In the threatening postures the horse lowers its head, pins back its ears and bares its teeth or it will swiftly turn its hindlegs towards an enemy or rival and lash out with its heels.

Two horses (*far right*) find out if they know each other while companions use one another as rubbing posts (*below and below right*).

Manoeuvrability and agility, often linked with speed, are the horse's natural means of defence. These are the basic qualities that man has exploited for his own needs since he first domesticated the horse.

The gallop symbolizes the spirit of the horse, the spirit of freedom and open spaces. It is the fastest of the horse's natural paces and is one of the horse's four natural gaits.

It is possible for the horse to vary any of the four gaits to control its balance and locomotion: for example, the ordinary walk and the extended walk, the ordinary trot and the extended trot and so on. Full advantage is taken of these paces in the training of riding horses. The horse's natural instinct is to run with the herd and this can be seen in the Thoroughbred on the racetrack. Thoroughbreds, a man-made breed, are produced for speed and stamina but one of the fastest horses over short distances is the American Quarter Horse. The breeds shown here at full stretch are wild Dulmen ponies (*below*); Lipizzaners (*previous page*); and Thoroughbreds (*opposite and bottom picture*).

Mares and foals

Four mares; four foals; and, perhaps, four more foals on the way. Mares have most chance of conceiving just after giving birth. The wild pony (*opposite, top right*) that has the freedom to run her own breeding programme, will certainly have mated with a stallion shortly after foaling. The activities of the others depend on the programmes drawn up by the stud-farms on which they live.

Foals are usually born just over 11 months after conception, although mares often surprise their owners by giving birth a whole month earlier (or later).

Like many other animals that are born in the open in their wild state, a new-born foal can see, hear, and, after a very short while, stand up. Its first movements are always made in the direction of food; it wobbles its way along its mother's side until it can find her udder and attach itself hungrily.

While it is still very young, a foal will try to imitate its mother by grazing, but it is not able to chew grass until it is two months old. Weaning takes place between six and eight months; an older foal that tries to suckle may well find itself subject to heavy maternal discouragement.

In the foal stage, which lasts about a year, a horse is in its most playful period. Foals frolic, dance, engage in endless races with no starting-lines or winning posts. Very young ones often seem uncertain as to whether they want to go forwards or backwards. They also spar with each other. It is all good practice for being a competent, ready-to-run adult horse.

Familiar sights

The modern horse is transported in trailers or motor-horseboxes (*below*) but originally it was the horse that transported man and his goods along the trade routes and on journeys of exploration. Correctly handled horses adapt to modern transport conditions well and the equine millionaires of the racetrack are often flown in big jet-planes to race in another continent or to stand at stud. International show jumpers, too, are seasoned travellers, often competing in America one week and in Europe the next.

Thirsty horses at their trough (*right*) are a familiar sight to country-dwellers. Such sights used to be familiar to town-dwellers, too, and some cities still retain large kerb-side troughs that were set up during the last century for watering the hard-worked horses that pulled carriages, tradesmen's vans, carts and the early omnibuses. Often stationed at the tops of hills, these troughs were an indirect effect of the huge success that greeted Anna Sewell's *Black Beauty*, which roused public sympathy on behalf of working horses.

The horses shown here live a life vastly removed from that of a 19th century carter's pony. But, like every horse in every age, they still need a good supply of fresh, clean water.

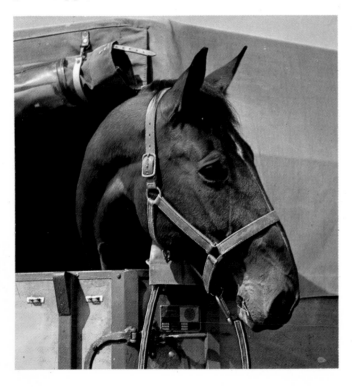

Less familiar sights

The tethered Mongolian ponies with their backs
to the wind (*below*) are thought to be
descendants of a strain of Asiatic steppe ponies
that survived the Ice Age. Although not as sleek
nor as handsome as the Arab or Thoroughbred,
the Mongolian pony is tough with great powers
of endurance. It can live and thrive on rough
foods and in climates that would not support the
finer strains of horses.

Turkish nomad women (*opposite*) dismantle a
water skin while the horse, on which the
nomads' way of life depends, allows itself to be
haltered. The donkey in the background is used
mainly as a pack animal.

The horse is a creature of habit and thrives on routine. This is the first basic principle of good horse-care, and management should be geared to keeping feed-times, riding-out and work-out periods to roughly the same time each day. The second basic principle of good management is to handle horses quietly and positively.

Housing

There are two types of housing suitable for horses and ponies – the traditional loose-box and the open-plan horse-barn. With both systems the essential requirements are enough room, light, ventilation and a dry, warm surface. Whichever system is used the floor area, which should be well drained, must be at least 4m × 3·5m (14ft × 12ft) for a horse and for the average pony 3·5m × 3m (12ft × 10ft) with a door width of 1·2m (4ft) and a height clearance that allows the animal entrance and exit without lowering its head. The doors of loose-boxes should be in two portions, the lower equipped with double bolts.

Straw is the best form of bedding. Wheat straw is the superior as it is easy to handle, drains well and looks bright and warm. Wood shavings or chippings and sawdust used together or separately make a cheap, efficient form of bedding.

All loose-boxes or stalls should be mucked out (cleaned out) daily and the bedding replenished with fresh material. During the working day, any droppings should be removed regularly.

Living-out

Horses or ponies living-out at grass need about 1 acre per pony and 2 acres per horse. In the southern hemisphere even clean-breds can live-out all year, and a south-facing open-fronted shelter is required.

Grooming

The objectives of grooming, or more accurately strapping, are to promote health, to maintain condition and prevent disease, especially skin problems, to ensure cleaniness and to improve appearance.

Strapping can be overdone particularly with the competition clean-bred or Thoroughbred horse and pony. They are thinner skinned than other equines and too much brushing will only make them irritable instead of promoting health. The best system is to quarter in the mornings before schooling or a work-out and strap in the afternoons when the horse has relaxed. Quartering is simply a general clean-up first thing in the morning. The horse is tied-up in its stall with its night rugs removed. In colder climates it is better to simply fold up the night rug over the horse's body so that it is partially covered throughout the operation. Any dirt or straw marks are brushed out with a body brush; hay or straw in the mane or tail are taken out by hand; and the eyes, nostrils and dock are gently sponged clean. The feet are then picked out and greased with hoof-oil which is applied to the soles of the feet and the walls. The water brush is then used to give the final touches by dampening down the mane and tail. The horse is then ready to be tacked-up for work or exercise.

The full strapping operation should take about 30 to 45 minutes. Again the horse should be tied-up in its stall with its day rugs completely or partially removed. The first operation is to pick out the feet with a hoof pick which should be used with the blunt point moving away from the sensitive skin of the horse's heels. The horse's feet should have been washed after exercise or work. This makes a good daily opportunity for checking the state of the horse's feet and shoes. The old saying 'no feet, no horse' is one of the most sensible in horse management. A dandy brush is then used to brush out dirt deposits and sweat marks especially in the saddle, girth and bridle areas.

softer body brush should be used for the belly, flanks, under the forearm and around the ears. Then it is the turn of the body brush which is not just for cleaning but also for massaging the muscles. This should be used in a semi-circular motion with a curry comb being used at about every third or fourth stroke to clean out the brush. The body brush is used in the left-hand when working from the near-side (left) of the horse and in the right-hand when working from the off-side (right). The dandy brush should never be used on the mane and tail but the soft body brush can be used on the mane. A damp sponge is then used to clean out, gently, the corners and perimeter of the eyes, the nostrils, lips and dock region. The final stage is to grease the feet with hoof-oil which promotes horn growth. The horse or pony is then ready for rugging-up for the night.

Horse clothing

A variety of blankets and rugs are made for different purposes. Night and day rugs, blankets and exercise sheets should be used according to the prevailing conditions.

Feeding

Feeding the horse is quite a science and what to feed depends upon several factors, such as the work it is going to do, its temperament, its breeding and its size. In general terms the following guide lines should be followed:

1. Keep the feeding programme as near to the natural method as possible, in other words feed little and often.
2. Feed plenty of bulk foods such as hay. This will act as a substitute for natural grazing.
3. Keep the feed measures in relation to the work done. For example, a competition horse standing 15hh and upwards, 6·3kg (14 lbs) of oats should be given, over the number of feeds given daily. All feeds for horses and ponies should be mixed with top quality bran and chaff (chopped hay). Feed a competition pony standing 14.2hh, 1·3 to 2·3kg (3 to 5 lb) of oats spread over two feeds daily (use Pony Cubes in the other feeds). Feed a child's riding pony standing 13.2hh, 1·8kg (4lb) of Pony Cubes per day. Mixed-in sliced carrots can be fed to give variety.

4. Fresh clean water should be available to the horse or pony at all times.

For the grass-kept animal the herbage should be even over the paddock, succulent and well coloured. Fresh water or a running stream should be easily available. In severe weather or when the grass is not growing at least two feeds a day and hay should be given.

Exercise

The object of exercise is to build and maintain condition. The programme must be planned to build up progressively, starting with a short period each day at a slow pace with plenty of active walking and slow trotting over fairly flat terrain. As the horse gets fitter so the exercise periods and their pace can be increased. The handler will be able to judge the horse's progress to fitness by the rhythm of its breathing. The harder the horse gets, the less he will blow.

The object of work-outs or schooling sessions is to educate, render supple and prepare the horse mentally for a specific competition. For example, the dressage competition horse would be worked to a programme exercising its body, learning new movements and improving responses to its rider's aids. A show jumper's work would be orientated to improving balance on the flat as well as accuracy in jumping. An eventing horse would be worked in dressage, jumping, both natural and unnatural obstacles, and suppling exercises. The art of work-outs or schooling is to keep the horse happy by keeping a good balance between repetition and boredom.

WORK HORSES

Industrialization has made scenes like these rare in the world today but there are still some countries and regions where the horse serves man in haulage and agriculture. In countries where horse power has been replaced with mechanical power, strength is still measured in horsepower.

Pack horses and ponies, like the one below, donkeys, asses and mules have been used for thousands of years. In parts of central Europe pack-horses or mules are still the best method of moving goods over rough or mountainous terrain.

The agricultural horse is a comparatively recent development. In the past, such work was always done by oxen and, in some parts of the world, it still is.

In the 19th century, however, farmers began to breed heavy horses like the one opposite (*below*) specifically for agriculture and, as a result, farming became more efficient.

The biggest of all draught horses, the British Shire (*top left*), weighs over a ton and can pull a load several times its own weight. Shires can stand as high as 18 hands; the equally famous Clydesdales are slightly smaller. Other giant horses include the French Boulonnais (16 hands) and Poitevin (17 hands), the Rhineland Heavy Draught of Germany (17 hands), the Dutch Draught (16.3 hands) and the Brabant (17 hands).

Cow ponies

The stockman (*opposite*) is rounding up fighting bulls in Andalusia. He is mounted on a Spanish horse which wears a bitless bridle. The Spanish breed of horses, with the warm blood of Eastern stallions running through their veins, are intelligent, agile horses, quick to learn the movements and airs of classical *haute école*.

The North American pioneers found that they had unexpectedly inherited some quality horses left behind by earlier Spanish explorers. These they crossed with clean-bred stallions imported from England, and with each subsequent generation they produced strains of superior types of versatile horse to work on the ranches.

Rodeo (*below*) is now one of North America's largest spectator sports. The word rodeo comes from the Spanish word *rodear*, meaning to go around. First used as a term for the round-up of cattle it was soon adapted as a name for the spectacle where cowboys and their ponies show their skills. Before mechanization, scenes similar to this steer roping would have been part of the cowboy and his Quarter Horse's or Cutting Horse's daily life.

The cowboy horse of the West is traditionally the Quarter Horse although the breed originated on the Eastern seabord of the USA. In Canada farm people use the Cutting Horse.

SPORT AND SHOW HORSES

The Thoroughbred, the Hunter, the Trotter, the native
ponies of Britain and the sharp little horses of China and
Mongolia have one thing in common. Like the showjumpers
below and opposite and the grey team overleaf, each plays
some part in the various forms of equestrian sport. Some,
like the Thoroughbred and the Standardbred, have
been developed for a specialized sport; others are equally
at home in a variety of roles. A top racehorse or
international showjumper can command a huge price on
the world bloodstock markets, while others have often been
purchased at a country sale for very little money.

Racing

Horse-racing is one of the most popular spectator sports in the world and has developed in many countries into a multi-million dollar gambling industry. The names of great racetrack performers like Ireland's Arkle, Britain's Mill Reef, America's Seattle Slew and Australia's Balmerino are as well known as any film star.

Organized racing, as we know it, was started in 16th-century England with meetings at York in the north and Chester in the north west. In the 17th century Charles II created the Round Course at Newmarket, now the headquarters of British racing. In 1752 the Jockey Club was first established and in 1791 the General Stud Book was published by Mr Weatherby. The British pattern of racing soon spread around the world. Internationally, the most popular and the richest form of the sport is flat-racing: the scene below is at America's Hialeah racetrack.

Harness-racing (*below*) actually originated in Norfolk, eastern England and was taken to the US by the early British settlers. America now is looked upon as the home of harness-racing but the sport is immensely popular in many countries. The sport has developed its own strains of throughbred horses.

Another variation of flat racing is steeplechasing. Steeplechasing came from the English hunting field. Although many countries stage hurdle racing, steeplechasing or hunt racing at a national level remains English (*bottom*).

Hunting

Hunting is one of the oldest equestrian sports. The ancient Assyrians hunted lions, wild bulls and even wild horses from horseback but it was in 17th-century Britain that organized hunting as we know it started.

Unlike flat racing, it was not royal influence that got the sport underway, but an accidental result of improved farming methods. In the 17th and 18th centuries, the disappearance of huge tracts of forest destroyed the essentially woodland sport of stag-hunting, and another quarry was needed to take its place. The fox – inedible, but a fast runner and an agricultural pest – was the chosen successor.

Even then, foxhunting did not immediately take on the fast pace it has today; huntsmen tended to jump their fences from a standstill rather than to a gallop. But dash gradually became the fashion, and with it came a need for horses that had the speed, the stamina and, above all, the strength to carry a rider like the huntsman opposite (*below right*) for hours without tiring. The hunter – not so much a breed as a type – was born.

Modern hunters span the whole range of horse breeds, with the Thoroughbred at one end and native ponies like the Welsh and the Exmoor at the other. But hunters strong enough to carry a heavy man are now in short supply, and command high prices.

Hunts like the Pytchley (*below*) and the Belvoir (*opposite, top*) are a traditional part of the British rural scene (there are some 200 foxhound packs in Britain), and similar scenes can be seen in America, Australia and New Zealand.

Schooling

Patient training methods dating back to the days of active cavalry have been used to encourage this Hungarian horse (*right*) to lie down on command. The same principles govern the handling of Lipizzaner stallions seen below in training at their stud in Lipizza. The precise classical riding of the 16th and 17th centuries can still be seen at the chanderliered Spanish Riding School in Vienna.

Although the Lipizzaner is perhaps the best known of *haute école* horses through the many foreign tours of the Spanish Riding School, other breeds such as the Thoroughbred, Hanoverian and Trakehner also excel at competitive dressage.

The word *dressage* means training the riding horse to its full physical and mental ability with suppleness and complete obedience to its rider. The word comes from the French verb *Dresser* and first came into use in the English language during the 16th century when it was correct *to dress* a riding horse and *train* a racehorse (then known as a running horse). Dressage should not be confused with *haute école*, a system of training that borders on the realms of the circus.

In modern equitation, dressage is the foundation of all the basic training given to a riding horse no matter what its uses may be at maturity. It is also a form of competition where horse and rider are tested at various levels of training in suppleness and obedience. Although basically a European sport, competitive dressage is becoming more popular than ever in America and Australia.

RIDING AND DRIVING

Top equestrian skills take much practice and hard work but
horses can be a way of life, whether they are driven in
matched pairs like the team shown below, or ridden
like the mounts of the two *gardiens* or cattleherds (*right*)
shown in the coastal marshes of the French Camargue.

Driving in style: four Welsh cobs in action at Britain's Cirencester Park. The skills involved in driving a horse-drawn vehicle are even older than those involved in riding. Men were driving carts, and war chariots, 4000 years ago.

Holidays on horseback (*top left*): with the Breton landscape spread out below them, three young riders and their horses let themselves go. It is a scene that is repeated thousands of times every year in holiday centres across the world. Organized horseback holidays, involving anything from a week's riding and camping to a daily hour or so of hacking, are a recent innovation, and are tremendously popular. They can be adapted to most levels of horsemanship, and to most ages: the children (*below*) on their sedate ponies are taking part in a pony-trek, or pony-walk.

Especially at the trekking level, sure-footed native ponies are particularly well suited to playing the key role in horseback holidays. The British Welsh, Fell, and Highland ponies are outstandingly good. Going further north, the native pony of Iceland is even better. The Icelandic is the direct descendant of ponies taken over to Iceland by the Vikings a thousand years ago. In addition to the normal horse gaits, they have a speciality of their own: the tølt, or fast amble. The tølt is pronounced extremely comfortable by those who have tried it. As a bonus, the Icelandic is almost in the racing-pigeon class when it comes to finding its own way home.

Not surprisingly, Iceland is a great centre for horseback holidays; others are Ireland, the Western United States, Germany and the United Kingdom (especially Wales).

Compared with riding, driving a horse or a team is a rare experience today. Yet the skill required and the pleasure to be gained should not be overlooked. Opposite the Clydesdale, Caesar of Shergold, waits for the judges at a British show. This is just one example of the type of vehicle and mode of harness which can be used.

Horse sports with a difference: above, Afghan horsemen come together in a spirited bout of 'catch the goat' or *baz-kiri*. The game is played rather like rugby football: the goat (a dead one) stands in for the ball, and the aim of each rider is to wrest it from his opponents and race with it towards a goal. Since the goat is often dropped, the sport calls for frequent daredevil swoops from the saddle, with the rider holding on by stirrups and will-power. The skill involved is obvious, as is the degree of horsemanship that allows both rider and mount to emerge from the game unscathed. *Baz-kiri* is played at full pelt and lasts for hours. Such conditions show the native abilities of the riders' horses at their full advantage.

There is another equestrian sport which takes a similar form to 'catch-the-goat' and that is,

of course, polo. Played with a ball instead of a carcass, polo dates back at least 2000 years and, like *baz-kiri*, has its roots firmly in the East. It first came to Europe from India, where the British soldiers and civilians of the Raj discovered it being played in Assam. Although the long mallet-like sticks used in the game cut out the need for those out-of-the-saddle swoops in *baz-kiri* style, play is still fast and potentially dangerous.

The players are kitted out in pads and safety-helmets, and the polo ponies' legs are also padded. All horses used in polo are called ponies, whatever their size. Today, the majority are Argentinian bred.

The horse *opposite* is an Afghanistan Kabardin, born in the royal stud-farm at Kabul.

BREEDS

The modern world possesses well over a hundred horse and pony breeds: domestic and wild, cold-blooded and warm-blooded, large and small, heavy and light. The Belgian farm-horse, below, demonstrates the heavy draught type; the Lipizzaner, opposite, is built on much lighter lines.

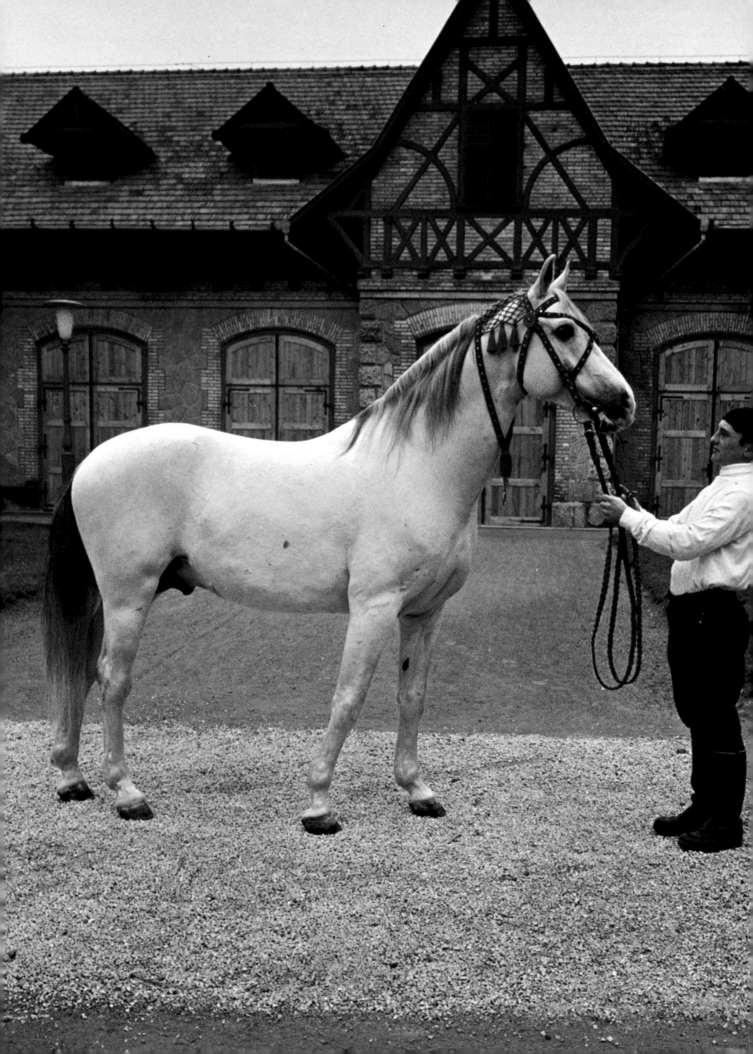

According to legend, there was once a lion which boasted it could see better than a horse. The horse disagreed, so they decided to put their powers to the test. The lion proved its skill by spotting a white pearl floating in a white bowl full of milk. The test given to the horse also involved a pearl, but a black one; it was set in a lump of coal. The horse saw it at once, and the lion was forced to concede the victory to his opponent.

The legend is Arabian, and the horse involved, naturally, is the Arab, whose powers of sight, speed and stamina are indeed near-legendary. The Arab is the oldest pure breed of horse in the world. Its origins are uncertain, but its bloodlines have been recorded back as far as the sixth century A.D. Still bred according to fanatical standards of purity by the Arabs themselves, it has by now bequeathed some of its unique character and physique to almost all the well-known breeds we have today. The half-bred horse (*opposite*) in a European stud-farm shows just how strongly an Arab can set its stamp on his immediate descendants.

The most famous breed with Arab blood in its veins is probably the British Thoroughbred. Every modern Thoroughbred is descended from one of three Arabs that lived in the 17th and 18th centuries. The earliest was the Byerley Turk. Next came the Darley Arabian and then the Godolphin Arabian (said to have been discovered pulling a water-cart in Paris) made its appearance. Other breeds that have felt the Eastern influence are the Lipizzaner, the South American Criollo, the German Trakehner, the Hungarian Nonius, the Polish Wielkopolski and the Australian Waler. Hungary and Poland also breed Arabian strains of their own, while the British Anglo-Arab is the result of an Arab-Thoroughbred cross.

The elegant American Saddle Horse (*left*) stems from homely beginnings. The breed began as a speedy and comfortable means of transport for plantation-owners with big estates. Its place of origin is indicated by its earlier name: the Kentucky Saddler. Today, it is seen mainly in the show ring, where particularly talented individuals show off no less than five gaits: the walk, the trot, the canter, the prancing slow-gait and the much faster rack. A relative is the Tennessee Walking Horse, with its unusual running walk.

Saddle Horses have a mixture of Thoroughbred and Morgan blood in their veins; a Morgan is shown below. Another American breed, Morgans get their name from the very first horse of their line, a Vermont-born foal called Justin Morgan. No one has ever been able to work out Justin Morgan's pedigree; but Justin himself, in spite of his mysterious background, grew up to found a line of brilliant harness racers and, later, saddle horses. He is unique in that no other horse has ever had the honour of having a breed named after him.

Although the horse species originated in North America, all the American horses of today are ultimately derived from Old World breeds. As has been stated the last wild horses of the original American stock died out about 10,000 years ago and the reasons for this are still a mystery.

The complex history of the Appaloosa (*below*) is a typical example of the way modern American breeds emerged from their Old World backgrounds. At the furthest end of the Appaloosas' line stands a group of Spanish horses that were shipped across the Atlantic in the 1500s during the European conquest of Central America. (Another spotted breed, the Danish Knabstrup, also has Spanish blood.) Some were bought or stolen by Indians living in what are now the southernmost states of the USA and, of these, some again made their way north to the Nez Percé Indian territory of the

Palouse Valley in Idaho. The Nez Percés used their acquisitions as the foundation for a breed of war-horses. The breed's name derives from the name of the valley where it was born.

The characteristics that the Indians encouraged in their spotted fighting horses – speed, staying power and a good disposition – are those that have brought the Appaloosa into high demand as a saddle horse today. And, like the Danish Knabstrup, the Appaloosa is also in demand as a circus horse; the reason is its distinctive spotted coat. Several patterns are allowed and include the 'leopard' (dark spots on white) and the 'snowflake' (pale spots on a dark coat, usually roan). The mare below has a 'leopard' coat. Similar patterns are permitted on the new pony breed, the Pony of the Americas, or POA for short. The POA came into being in 1954, from a Shetland/Appaloosa cross. It is very popular as a child's mount.

A true horse breed – or just a colour variety? Most admirers of the blond-maned Palomino (*below*) are not too worried on this point: for them, the horse is simply one of the most handsome the world has ever seen. But the question does worry experts, and for a good reason.

As with all domestic animals, a distinctive line of horses has to breed true to type over several generations before it can be called a breed. But the Palomino – whose distinction lies in its colour – does not. A breeder who mates two Palominos cannot be sure that the result will be a Palomino foal – although the foal itself, when adult, could well sire a Palomino in its turn. At the moment, Palomino colouring can appear in several true horse breeds, including the Arab and the American Quarter Horse.

Overleaf: The origin of all the nursery rocking horses in the world is the dappled Percheron, a draught horse with a trace of Arab blood. It is named after its home district in France, the Perche.

A herd of Camarguais (*far right*) known as the 'wild horses of the sea'. This ancient breed that lives in the desolate marsh region at the mouth of the Rhône in southern France descended from the Solutrean 'ram-headed' horse.

The ram-shaped head of the Camargue horse (*top right*) is very distinctive. These horses are semi-wild and are now mainly a tourist attraction, although at one time they were used as stock horses, and on rare occasions are used today in that role. The Gardiens, a type of French wrangler, used them for working with the black fighting bulls of the Camargue. It is thought that they are the forerunner of the modern North African Barb.

The Mongolian or Asiatic Wild Horse (*bottom right*) is thought to be the most ancient breed of horse in the world today. The breed was discovered in 1881 by the Russian explorer Colonel N. M. Przewalski. Asiatic Wild are small and are usually bay or dun in colour with a distinctive dorsal stripe. There are some 200 of these horses now in zoos around the world but the largest herd is in Prague where a stud book on the breed is also kept.

The Trakehner (*far right below*) is one of Europe's most popular and versatile sporting horses. The famous Trakehner Stud was founded in 1732 by Frederick William I of Prussia using mares and stallions of various breeds. With the passing of generations the quality of the breed was improved with the injection of Eastern and Thoroughbred blood. One horse in particular had a marked influence on the breed, the Thoroughbred stallion Perfectionist (by the great racehorse Persimmon). He stood at the stud for three breeding seasons and left 32 stallions and 37 brood mares out of 131 of his foals. The Trakehner, also known as the East Prussian, is now bred extensively in West Germany. The powers of endurance of the breed were proved during World War II when a group of Trakehners from their East Prussian stud trekked 900 miles westwards to safety through the depths of a central European winter. Their extraordinary journey took them three months. The Trakehners have since shown top-class ability in the modern worlds of show-jumping, three-day eventing and competition dressage.

INDEX

**This edition published in 1981
by Cathay Books
59 Grosvenor Street, London W1**

ISBN 0 86178 102 3

© 1979 Octopus Books Limited

Produced by
Mandarin Publishers Limited
22a Westlands Road
Quarry Bay, Hong Kong

Printed in Hong Kong

PDO 81-161